The Ni-Go Project: The History and Legacy of Imperial Japan's Nuclear Weapons Program during World War II

By Charles River Editors

The Institute of Physical and Chemical Research building in Taisho period

About Charles River Editors

Charles River Editors provides superior editing and original writing services across the digital publishing industry, with the expertise to create digital content for publishers across a vast range of subject matter. In addition to providing original digital content for third party publishers, we also republish civilization's greatest literary works, bringing them to new generations of readers via ebooks.

Sign up here to receive updates about free books as we publish them, and visit Our Kindle Author Page to browse today's free promotions and our most recently published Kindle titles.

Introduction

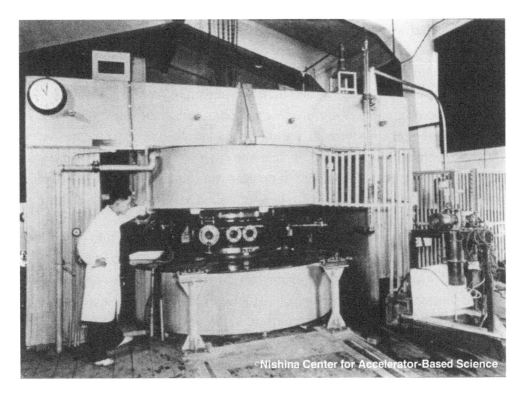

A RIKEN cyclotron

"What if the enemy should get the atomic bomb before we did! We could not run the mortal risk of being outstripped in this awful sphere." – Winston Churchill

Before the Second World War, military conflicts were fought under orthodox conditions, usually termed "conventional warfare," but several innovations had significantly changed combat, leading inextricably to the race for a nuclear weapon in the 1930s and 1940s. Conflicts had been fought by armies on horseback with guns of varying sophistication since the 16th century, but mechanized warfare and machine guns changed this calculus and set the stage for future combat by the end of World War I. Other sinister changes entered the fray during this conflict, such as chemical weapons like chlorine and mustard gas. The total warfare brought about by World War I and ensuing wars like the Spanish Civil War made the quest for the most powerful weapons somewhat necessary.

Tens of millions died during World War II as the warring powers raced to create the best fighter planes, tanks, and guns, and eventually that race extended to bombs which carried enough power to destroy civilization itself. While the war raged in Europe and the Pacific, a dream team of Nobel Laureates was working on the Manhattan Project in America, a program kept so secret that Vice President Harry Truman didn't know about it until he took the presidency after FDR's death in April 1945.

The Manhattan Project would ultimately yield the "Little Boy" and "Fat Man" bombs that released more than 100 Terajoules of energy at Hiroshima and Nagasaki, but as it turned out, the Axis were not far behind with their own nuclear weapons program. When the Nazis' quest for a nuclear weapon began in earnest in 1939, no one really had a handle on how important nuclear weapons would prove to war and geopolitics. The attacks on Hiroshima and Nagasaki in August 1945, along with the Cold War-era tests and their accompanying mushroom clouds, would demonstrate the true power and terror of nuclear weapons, but in the late 1930s these bombs were only vaguely being thought through, particularly after the successful first experiment to split the atom by a German scientist. The nuclear age itself was in its infancy, barely 35 years old, but within a few short years the advent of nuclear war loomed over the world and the prospect of the enemy winning the nuclear race kept Allied leaders awake at night.

In November 1921, roughly a year after the Treaty of Versailles came into effect, Japan, Britain, and the United States gathered to sign another treaty of disarmament at the Washington Naval Conference. However, Japan opted against renewing the pact in the mid-1930s, and around the same time, Germany openly breached the terms of the former treaty and began to restock their weapons. This gave rise to the birth of a new and unprecedented arms race, one that had catastrophically disastrous consequences about a decade later.

Although their project is typically overlooked given the American use of the bombs and then the Soviets following suit early on in the Cold War, the Japanese avidly pursued nuclear weapons as well. *The Ni-Go Project: The History and Legacy of Imperial Japan's Nuclear Weapons Program during World War II* examines Japan's race to reach the ultimate goal during the war, how they went about their objectives, and why they failed. Along with pictures of important people, places, and events, you will learn about Japan's nuclear weapons program like never before.

The Ni-Go Project: The History and Legacy of Imperial Japan's Nuclear Weapons Program during World War II

The Tug of War

The invention of the atomic bomb is one of the prime examples of how science, one of the most powerful and indispensable tools at people's disposal, can lead to fruitful innovations and life-changing discoveries, but also evil and ruination. This vicious contrivance was not created overnight. Quite the contrary, it was a piecemeal process that can be traced back as early as 1789, when German chemist Martin Heinrich Klaproth discovered a mysteriously dense, metallic element which he called "uranium," christened after the planet Uranus. The French-Polish physicist Madame Marie Curie began her seminal research on the element and its radioactivity, caused by atomic decay, 107 years later. In 1911, the New Zealand-born physicist Ernest Rutherford achieved yet another milestone when he produced the first model of the atom, and he split the atom at the University of Manchester six years later, thereby becoming the first individual to create an artificial nuclear reaction.

The scientific breakthroughs of the first decades of the 20th century would play a vital role. In October 1933, the Hungarian-German physicist Leo Szilard was credited with developing the concept of self-sustaining nuclear fission reactions, otherwise known as a "nuclear chain reaction." Five years later, German physicist Otto Hahn, with the assistance of his research partner Fritz Strassmann and the theoretical expertise of Hahn's niece Lise Meitner, split the atom for the first time in history on December 17, 1938 in Berlin. A uranium isotope - Uranium 235 - was bombarded by neutrons, causing it to become highly unstable. Temporarily becoming a separate version of the isotope, it released a large amount of energy when split, and the reaction became known as nuclear fission. The following excerpt spelled out the effects of uranium fission in layman's terms, as summarized by Canadian scientist and nuclear consultant Dr. Gordon Edwards: "When a uranium atom splits, it gives off more neutrons, which can then split more atoms, and so the energy level rapidly multiplies."

Hahn

Meitner

It did not take long for the scientists to realize that they had potentially unlocked Pandora's Box, and they soon began to fret over the irrevocable ramifications of their discoveries. Szilard, who partnered with Canadian-American physicist Walter Zinn and succeeded in recreating Meitner and Hahn's uranium fission experiment a few months later, made this sobering remark: "That night, there was very little doubt in my mind that the world was headed for grief." He elaborated on his concerns in a letter to President Franklin D. Roosevelt, which he co-authored with Albert Einstein in August 1939: "This new phenomenon would also lead to the construction of bombs, and it is conceivable...that extremely powerful bombs of a new type may thus be constructed."

Upon learning about these major breakthroughs, national leaders around the world sprang into action at once, working on curating the uranium and plutonium needed to develop the world's first atomic bomb. Among them was Roosevelt himself, who approved the infamous Manhattan Project that same year, a $2.2 billion undertaking that was comprised of more than 30 project sites manned by over 130,000 scientists. Unsurprisingly, the implications of detonating this revolutionary explosive were not lost on the theoretical physicist Julius Robert Oppenheimer from the University of California, Berkeley, who was among those recruited to helm this colossal venture and is most often recognized as the inventor of the atomic bomb.

Oppenheimer and Einstein

When the heads of the Manhattan Project gathered in Alamogordo, New Mexico on July 16, 1945, to observe the first successful test of the atomic bomb, code name "Trinity," Oppenheimer quoted a chilling line from the *Bhagavad Gita:* "Now I am become Death, the destroyer of worlds." The 19-kiloton blast from the plutonium-based bomb, nicknamed "Gadget," produced a blinding mushroom cloud that rocketed 40,000 feet into the air and left behind an enormous crater stretching more than 300 meters wide.

That may have been the first nuclear weapon detonated, but the major world powers had been scrambling for years to get ahead in the nuclear arms race. Although their project is typically overlooked given the American use of the bombs and then the Soviets following suit early on in the Cold War, the Japanese avidly pursued nuclear weapons as well.

The complex modern history of Japan – particularly during the final years of feudal rule upheld by its military dictators, the Tokugawa shoguns, to the re-establishment of the empire following the Meiji Restoration in 1868 – was largely characterized by volatility and instability. In addition to grappling with bloody domestic disputes and turbulent bouts of civil unrest for centuries on end, Japanese leaders dealt with repeated attempts of foreign intervention. Japan experienced the first serious instance of unwelcome Western interference towards the end of the Tokugawa (or Edo) era, a period known as *"Bakumatsu,"* as dubbed by the locals.

In the spring of 1854, Commodore Matthew C. Perry of the US Navy, with the aid of his striking squadron of eight all-black warships, triumphantly pressured the Tokugawan officials into signing the Kanagawa Treaty under threat of force. As per the treaty's terms, Japan was made to open the ports of Hakodate and Shimoda to American merchant vessels, thus quashing the state's previously untouched 214-year-old tradition of national isolation, otherwise known as "*sakoku*." Apart from forging diplomatic and exclusive trade relations with the US, Japanese officials were also forced to sanction the post of an American consul, as well as an embassy, and promised to extend its protection to all American visitors and castaways. Four years later, Japan grudgingly signed a second covenant entitled the "Treaty of Amity and Commerce (US-Japan)," AKA the "Harris Treaty," which opened up the ports of Kanagawa, Nagasaki, Niigata, Hyogo, and later, those at Tokyo, Kobe, and Yokohama to international trade.

The highly unpopular treaties played an instrumental role in the collapse of the Tokugawa shogunate and the subsequent rise of the Meiji era, during which the emperor was reinstated as the supreme ruler of the state. Meiji reformers lambasted the shoguns and Edo officials for kowtowing to the unconscionable demands and strong-arm tactics of the Americans, which they claimed was a belligerent attack against Japanese independence. They vigorously voiced their fears over being reduced to a Western colony, a fate that had befallen China, India, and other parts of Southeast Asia. As such, the policies instituted by the new administration were built upon their quest to restore Japanese sovereignty and reinforce the empire's dominance in the hopes of creating a powerful, autonomous state on par with those in the West. These sentiments were encapsulated in the Meiji slogan: "*fukoku kyohei*," which translates to "enrich the country [and] strengthen the army."

To reclaim their economic self-sufficiency, the Meiji administration took great steps to remodel and industrialize the empire, primarily via the introduction of capitalism. Along with dismantling merchant guilds, internal checkpoints, and outdated courier postal stations in favor of modern post offices, imperial officials invested heavily in renovating their major roads, expanding their existing infrastructure, and building brand-new public facilities. The first telegraph line between Tokyo and Yokohama was installed in 1869, Japan's telegraph network continued to scale up in the years that followed, and the Japanese soon boasted underwater cables that connected Nagasaki to Shanghai. In 1872, Japan constructed its first railroad between Tokyo and Yokohama, and another line linking Kobe to Osaka was laid in 1874. The next year, the empire officially became a part of the Universal Postal Union and imported its first batch of telephones. Meiji officials also founded schools and academic institutions dedicated to the advancement of science and technology and provided capital for the construction of iron and steel manufacturing plants, shipbuilding factories, and coal mining companies.

Despite their patent distaste for Western intervention, Meiji officials understood that in order to propel themselves forward and be taken seriously as a formidable global power, they had to learn the tricks of the trade from their rivals. Thus, in 1871, a team of 50 academics from Iwakura

Tomomi were dispatched to the Europe and the United States, where they were tasked with studying the local political, educational, treaty, and banking systems for two years. In the same vein, Japanese scientists abroad were exposed to the scientific ideas and technological breakthroughs of their foreign peers, thus providing them with the knowledge needed to launch their nuclear weapons program in later years. Hundreds of Western professionals, referred to as the "*yatoi*," were also invited to Japan to teach English and science, edit newly founded English newspapers, and train local engineers on the construction of traditionally Western architecture and amenities. Professor James Huffman of Wittenburg University explained, "The new leaders studied Western models with a zeal born of deep fear that weakness might invite invasion."

By the end of the 19th century, the empire had transformed into a fully functioning, industrialized nation that was on part with the most advanced Western states. More notably, with the solid, modernized infrastructure that the empire now possessed, along with the rapid growth of their local industries and national institutions, the Japanese military was now capable of both shoring up its defenses and sharpening its offensive strategies.

Japan activated the next phase of its pursuit for global dominance by flexing its military muscles. Somewhat ironically, Japan mimicked Commodore Perry's use of gunboat diplomacy in their slow, but ultimately successful colonization of Korea, which they deemed a potential threat to the empire. They won the First Sino-Japanese War (1894-1895), a conflict that arose from a territorial dispute over the Korea. Not only did they retain their dominion over the peninsula, they also acquired the Pescadores Islands and Taiwan (formerly known as "Formosa"). They entered the Russo-Japanese War in 1904 and once again emerged victorious with their superior army and navy, consisting of 270,000 expertly trained troops the following year. As a result, they received the rights to southern Manchuria, as well as the southern half of Sakhalin island. With that victory, Japan officially became the first Asian nation to conquer a European power.

World War I allowed Japan to debut the full potential of their military prowess, specifically their air and naval forces, on the global stage for the first time. The empire fought alongside Britain, France, Russia, and Italy, collectively known as the Allied Powers, and eventually helped defeat the Central Powers of Germany, Bulgaria, Austria-Hungary, and the Ottoman Empire.

With yet another victory under their belt, Japan further expanded its sphere of influence in Asia and the Pacific. At the same time, this victory boosted its reputation as a worthy adversary among other major powers and ushered in another prosperous golden era of industrialization within the empire. 1,118 companies, which included the likes of Mitsubishi Motors, Subaru, and Nikon, among other icons in heavy machinery, were founded in 1917 alone, and profits soared as foreign demand for high-quality Japanese exports skyrocketed. The French, for instance, whose ship-building capabilities were crippled by the war, ordered a dozen destroyers from Japan that same year. The empire also received recurring orders of guns, howitzer canons, and ammunition from Russia. Two years later, Japan was named one of the "Big Five" of the new international order at the conference in Versailles, and Japan was formally inducted into the League of Nations. Jurgen Melzer, a contributor of the *International Encyclopedia of the First World War,* noted, "With its expansion into the Chinese mainland, the southern Pacific, and the Transbaikal region, the Japanese military eventually controlled an area nearly as vast as the World War II Pacific War theater."

Inevitably, Japan's aggressive colonialism and combative tactics would strain its already rocky relationship with the United States and Britain, both of whom owned significant stakes in China, Southeast Asia, and the Pacific, and things took a turn for the worse in the early 1920s. The empire suffered its first major blow at the 1922 Washington Conference, during which Japanese delegates reluctantly returned the Qingdao territory to China. At the same time, Japan signed the Five-Power Treaty, an agreement dictating that all participants restrict their naval construction in an effort to stymie the naval arms race and ensure peace. What's more, Britain caved into American demands and terminated the Anglo-Japanese alliance in June of the following year.

The loss of crucial allies and the empire's tumbling prestige aside, Japan was struck by a devastating 7.9-magnitude earthquake, which also created a cataclysmic tsunami in September 1923. Now remembered as the "Great Kanto Earthquake," the disastrous temblor claimed 142,800 lives, and along with the tsunamis and ensuing firestorms robbed 2.16 million residents in Tokyo and Yokohama of their homes. 7,000 factories, 121 bank head offices, 162 hospitals, and 117 primary schools were also reduced to rubble. At the time, it was the worst natural disaster in Japan's history.

Japan's train of misfortunes continued on into the next decade. The empire was not exempt from the Great Depression, experiencing its worst economic downturn between 1930 and 1932, which was exacerbated by the terrible famine that ravaged rural Japan two years later. In the meantime, the empire, struggling to regain its footing, invaded Manchuria and established the puppet state of Manchukuo in 1932. The League sided with China and recommended that Manchuria be re-instituted as a Chinese province. Predictably, Japan spurned the verdict and formally resigned from the League in March 1933, effectively distancing itself even further from its previous allies.

Deprived of access to crucial natural resources that could only be procured overseas, Japan occupied Burma, Guam, and a number of other American territories across Asia and the Pacific, which only inflamed tensions further between the sides. The United States retaliated by scrapping their 1911 commercial treaty with Japan in 1939, and in mid-October of 1940, Roosevelt sanctioned an embargo "on all exports of scrap iron and steel to destinations other than Britain and the nations of the Western Hemisphere." Roosevelt upped the ante once more in July 1941 when he froze all Japanese assets within the United States, shut down the Panama Canal to Japanese shipping, and imposed a second ban on the export of oil. With this embargo,

Japan would exhaust the entirety of its oil reserves within half a year. Likewise, British and Dutch officials prohibited all exports to Japan from their respective colonies in southeast Asia.

Japan found itself in crisis mode at this juncture. The survival of the empire's industrial sectors hinged on the coal, steel, iron ore, rubber, tin, copper, petroleum, and other raw materials imported from abroad. To put this into perspective, 93% of Japan's copper and nearly 75% of its scrap iron were shipped in from the United States. "Commercial and economic relations between Japan and third countries, led by England and the United States, are gradually becoming so horribly strained that we cannot endure it much longer," lamented Foreign Minister Teijiro Toyoda. "Consequently, our Empire, to save its very life, must take measures to secure the raw materials of the South Seas."

On September 27, 1940, the empire signed the Tripartite Pact, aligning itself with Germany and Italy and officially entering World War II.

Nishina and the Ni-Go Project

"The nuclear arms race is like two enemies standing waist-deep in gasoline, one with three matches, the other with five." - Carl Sagan, 20th century American astronomer

While Japan, like other major powers, was already in the process of sowing the seeds for their nuclear weapons program, it was upon their entry into the war that truly spurred the atomic bomb project. Given its fall from grace, which came on the heels of its fleeting global dominance, Japan was anxious to beef up its defenses and reclaim some former glory.

Perhaps the most notable forefather of the empire's controversial atomic bomb project was Hantaro Nagaoka, who is said to have been the first Japanese scientist to express a spirited interest in atomic physics. In 1900, the Nagasaki-born Nagaoka attended the Inaugural International Congress of Physicists in Paris, where he had the privilege of observing a lecture on radioactivity by Madame Curie herself. That presentation featured a stunning visual aid: a radium-infused sample bathed in an ethereal glow. In 1904, Nagaoka constructed a model of an atom containing a nucleus encircled by a Saturn-like ring of electrons, and in doing so he became the first in the field to suggest the presence of a nucleus in an atom, supposedly seven years before Rutherford's revelation. In fact, Rutherford later referenced Nagaoka's findings in the 1911 treatise he penned on his gold foil experiment.

Nagaoka

Nagaoka reached a new high in 1925 when he was made head scientist of the RIKEN Institute for Physical and Chemical Research, as well as Director of the Physics Division. This was a relatively new research complex situated in the city of Wako in the Saitama Prefecture, roughly 16 miles northwest of Tokyo, erected just eight years prior to his arrival. Nagaoka, however, made virtually no direct contributions to the country's budding nuclear weapons program, as he eventually left RIKEN and went on to serve as the first president of Osaka Imperial University, founded in 1931.

In 1934, three pioneering papers on atomic physics authored by a physics professor and research associate of Tohoku University named Tadayoshi Hikosaka were published in the Japanese scientific journal, *Kagaku*. In a nutshell, Hikosaka described in depth the "shell-like structures" of nuclei and revealed the massive energy potential that atomic nuclei possessed, which could be used to generate electrical power and construct powerful explosives. This was four years before Hahn's first successful attempt at nuclear fission, which means Hikosaka may have been the first to ponder the possibility of harnessing atomic energy for weapons. He almost certainly was the first Japanese scientist to do so.

Later that year, physics professor Seishi Kikuchi of Osaka Imperial University, who previously published a well-received dissertation on the disintegration of radium, built a working replica of the Cockroft-Walton generator (also referred to as a "multiplier") from scratch. This bulky contraption, first designed by physicists John Cockroft and Ernest Walton at the University of Cambridge, was essentially a voltage-multiplying electric circuit with a ladder-like series of interlocking capacitors and rectifier diodes that produced high-voltage direct currents derived from lower alternating currents. Cockroft and Walton had used the generator to power their particle accelerator and succeeded in accelerating protons to a voltage of 700kV, which was bombarded onto a lithium sample and transmuted into helium; this was the first instance of artificial nuclear disintegration in history. In addition to conducting multiple neutron-scattering experiments with his 600kV Cockroft-Walton multiplier, Kikuchi fashioned a cloud chamber to provide vapor-trail visuals for particle paths, and he concocted small batches of "deuterium oxide" (water in which hydrogen molecules are replaced with the deuterium isotope, mainly used as a moderator in nuclear reactors).

Around the same time, Bunsaku Arakatsu, then based in Taipei Imperial University, became the first Japanese physicist to induce an artificial disintegration of light nuclei with a particle accelerator that he had assembled himself. This was the first atomic nucleus collision experiment performed in Asia. Sometime afterward, Arakatsu determined that every Uranium-235 atom that undergoes nuclear fission generally produces 2.6 neutrons. He returned to Japan in 1936 and became a lecturer at his alma mater, Kyoto Imperial University, where he continued his research on atomic and nuclear physics.

While the foregoing figures paved the way for the formation of the empire's nuclear weapons program, it was Dr. Yoshia Nishina, Japan's foremost expert on experimental physics and nuclear science, who brought the ambitious project to life. Nishina was born into an affluent family in the small, fairly obscure town of Satosho in the Okayama prefecture, and as an electrical engineering student, he graduated with honors from Tokyo Imperial University in 1918. In 1921, he studied experimental techniques under the tutelage of Ernest Rutherford at the Cavendish Laboratory in the University of Cambridge, and he spent the next two years at the Georg August University of Gottingen and the Neils Bohr Institute in Copenhagen. Apart from working alongside Bohr himself, he became intimately acquainted with a number of specialists in the fields of theoretical and quantum physics, including Werner Heisenberg, Wolfgang Pauli, and Paul Dirac.

Nishina

Upon Nishina's return to Japan in 1928, he joined the burgeoning team at RIKEN and resumed his seminal research on atomic physics. A few months later, Nishina entered a collaborative partnership with Swedish physicist Oskar Klein and began a comprehensive investigation, utilizing the Dirac relativistic theory of electrons, on Compton scattering, or "the scattering of an X-ray by an electron." The following year, the pair devised the Klein-Nishina formula, which could be used to calculate the scattering cross-section of photons and illustrate the interactions between gamma rays and matter.

In 1931, Nishina was summoned to Kyoto Imperial University to deliver a 10-day course on quantum mechanics, methodically introducing the subject matter to the empire's scientists for the first time. During this time, Bohr, Francis William Aston, and several other illustrious physicists from Europe were also invited to Japan to share their knowledge with the students of Tokyo Imperial University. These exclusive lectures revolved around the discovery of brand-new elements such as Rhenium 75, Hafnium 72, and Masurium 43.

In autumn of the same year, Nishina unveiled RIKEN's first Nuclear Research Laboratory, which was built for the purpose of exploring cosmic rays and nuclear physics. It was there that the chief researcher became an invaluable mentor to a new generation of up-and-coming physicists, among them future Nobel Laureates Hideki Yukawa and Shinchiro Tomonaga, who had also attended his lectures on quantum physics. The universities at Kyoto and Osaka would also serve as two other major centers of nuclear research in Japan.

Three years later, Imperial Japanese Navy (IJN) officials became interested when they learned about Fermi's experimental work with neutrons. Fermi and his colleagues had bombarded 63 stable elements – including uranium, the heaviest of them all with an atomic number of 92 – with neutrons, as opposed to protons, and had reportedly created 37 new radioactive substances. In the process, they had also determined that carbon and hydrogen were the most potent moderators in decelerating the bombarding neutrons. Fermi's peers, however, were unable to reach a consensus regarding his findings. Some concluded that the resulting products were, in fact, "transuranic" (having a higher atomic number than uranium) elements, and those who disagreed argued that the chemical properties of the artificially produced substances were more akin to lighter elements. Concerned about the implications of Fermi's findings, the IJN financed an investigation into these experiments to ascertain whether this knowledge could be used in the construction of a super-explosive. Japanese scientists eventually disproved this theory, but the navy chose to remain vigilant and continued to tune in for updates in this sphere.

In 1935, Nishina began to assemble the first 26-inch cyclotron, originally designed by Ernest O. Lawrence in the University of Berkeley in 1930, and he completed the finishing touches the following year. The first working model of its kind in Japan, Nishina's cyclotron was a device that accelerated charged atomic and subatomic particles or ions into "high energies" via an alternating electric field. It was smaller than that of the 37-inch cyclotron in Berkeley, but it was a landmark achievement all the same, and Japanese scientists, including aspiring physicists across all local universities, were given unrestricted access to the sophisticated device, allowing the empire to forge ahead with its nuclear research more expeditiously.

In 1937, Nishina received word that Lawrence was in the midst of constructing a monstrous 60-inch cyclotron, otherwise known as the "California cyclotron," or "Calutron" for short. Keen to build one of his own, Nishina wrote to Lawrence and solicited his assistance in the construction of a duplicate at RIKEN. To Nishina's delight, Lawrence agreed and mailed him the tools and components required to build his own giant cyclotron in early 1938. One of the modules that Lawrence shipped over was a gargantuan 220-ton magnet, then the largest magnet in existence. Its great size, however, was misleading, as the magnet would only be capable of separating small quantities of Uranium-235 for research purposes; it was not powerful enough to process the kilograms needed to produce a weapon.

Meanwhile, a doctoral graduate from Tokyo University named Paul Kazuo Kuroda, another mentee of Nishina's at RIKEN, began to work on his dissertation on uranium purification. RIKEN researchers published a paper titled "Artificial Production of Uranium and Thorium" in *Nature* magazine in 1939, and in the next two years, they churned out four more supplementary papers on the subject which were jointly written by three physicists and two chemists. At this stage, mass spectometry pundit and Osaka University physics professor Tsunesaburo Asada was also commissioned to deliver a set of bimonthly lectures at the Naval Aeronautical Research Institute (NARI) in Yokosuka, as well as the Naval Technical Research Institute (NTRI) in Tokyo.

When Nishina, much like his contemporaries around the world, caught wind of Hahn's nuclear fission experiment in 1939, he instantly appreciated the gravity of this find and foresaw the commencement of the global nuclear arms race. He expressed to his colleagues his fear that major world powers, the United States specifically, had now embarked a mission to fabricate a nuclear weapon that could level entire cities in Japan. Nishina's concerns, as it turns out, were completely valid – just months later, Roosevelt started a chain of investigations into the development of fission explosives, which eventually evolved into the Manhattan Project. In fact, the Berkeley laboratory where Nishina had purchased parts for his reproduction of the Calutron became one of the primary sites of the American nuclear weapons program.

By then, Japan was already making decent headway in their nuclear research, but it was at this point that the empire's scientists began to exert more effort into forwarding their studies. That being said, the laboratories at RIKEN and the two universities were crudely equipped and meagerly staffed, particularly when compared to the resources available to American scientists. The number of Japanese particle physicists who could be classified as experts in this field was acutely limited, and few, apart from Nishina, were employed to tackle the atomic bomb project full-time. This glaring personnel shortage would prove to be one of Japan's greatest stumbling blocks, especially when there were tens of thousands of American scientists and technicians working around the clock in over two dozen research facilities across three cities in Tennessee, Washington, and New Mexico.

The lack of experience among the little manpower Japan had at hand served as yet another hindrance to the advancement of their nuclear program. Takeuchi Masa, one of Nishina's colleagues, spent 18 months developing a working thermal gaseous diffusion uranium-enrichment device, whereas the same apparatus was constructed in mere weeks in the United States.

Moreover, all American researchers were gifted housing, medical care, and a slew of other fringe benefits. Japanese scientists, on the other hand, as one shall soon see, struggled to secure stable funding and were continuously entangled in bureaucratic red tape. Consequently, the momentum of Japanese nuclear research, which was largely reliant on Nishina's team, was comparatively sluggish. It was only towards the final days of the war that Japanese researchers began to pick up the pace.

In the summer of 1940, Nishina and an unnamed colleague bumped into Lieutenant-General Takeo Yasuda, a trained electrical engineer who had been appointed director of the Army Aeronautical Technical Research Institute (AATRI) three years prior, on a train bound for

Tokyo. Nishina leapt on the opportunity to engage Yasuda in a discussion on nuclear fission, and he gauged the lieutenant-general's interest in officially launching a program geared towards the potential production of Japan's own nuclear weapon. Thoroughly impressed by Nishina's knowledge and prescience, Yasuda sent for Lieutenant-Colonel Tatsusaburo Suzuki, a fresh physics graduate from Tokyo University, and instructed him to assist Nishina's team in assessing the feasibility of constructing a uranium-based explosive.

Suzuki was sufficiently versed in X-rays and the ceramic pigmentation of uranium compounds, having studied these subjects at length at university, but he considered his grasp on general physics rudimentary. As such, he felt it wise to pick the brains of his former physics professor, Ryokichi Sagane, who had been a student of Lawrence's at Berkeley. Suzuki then put together a 20-page report for Yasuda in which he confirmed that Japan most likely possessed an adequate supply of uranium ore in their colonies abroad to develop what would become known as an atomic bomb. Lieutenant-Colonel Niizuma Seiichi, the director of the New Weapons department at the Bureau of Military Affairs, also voiced his support for the project.

In August, about a month after the chance encounter, a junior researcher and former Fermi associate named Tameichi Yazaki was sent to Berkeley on Nishina's behalf to gain a firmer understanding of cyclotron construction methods. Yazaki completed the task, returning a few weeks later with a stack of blueprints and a trove of technical tips. Back at RIKEN, researchers concluded, following several rounds of trial and error, that a nuclear fission chain reaction could not be achieved with natural uranium, and that only an enriched version (the process of artificially increasing the proportion of Uranium-235) of the substance would provide the desired effect.

For some reason, Suzuki's report, which he had submitted to his superior in October 1940, sat untouched on Yasuda's desk for several months. Yasuda finally got around to cracking the folder open in April 1941, and soon after, he rang up the Imperial Japanese Army's Minister of War and future Prime Minister Hideki Tojo. Yasuda presented Tojo with a proposal to launch the atomic bomb operation in an official capacity and received the general's blessing. Under Yasuda's instructions, Suzuki passed the message onto Viscount Masatoshi Okochi, the newly designated director of RIKEN. Okochi delivered the good news to Nishina personally, who was formally assigned to spearhead the venture. By then, Nishina's team consisted of a modest 100 or so researchers.

Tojo

With that, Nishina and his colleagues buckled down and plunged into their new, government-bankrolled enterprise with a spring in their steps. However, the construction of the Calutron was a far lengthier process than they had anticipated, and they were still hammering away on the project in December 1941, when 353 Japanese fighter jets and bombers decimated the US Naval Base at Pearl Harbor, killing about 2,400 sailors, soldiers, and civilians.

Around the same time, in the fall of 1940, Captain Yoji Ito of the NTRI took it upon himself to conduct an independent proof of concept study and evaluate if and how nuclear fission could be utilized by the navy. Like Suzuki, Ito deferred to Professor Sagane at Tokyo University for his professional opinion on the matter. Sagane, who was swamped with other work, only managed to submit his report to Ito in March 1942. Aside from listing the potential military applications for nuclear energy in his report, which included the possible installation of nuclear-powered weapons in Japanese warships, Sagane asserted that he was positive that American researchers had partnered with Jewish scientists who had fled Europe and were in the process of ramping up their research on atomic energy. Sagane strongly recommended that the empire take steps to speed up their own research, and he indirectly reaffirmed the need for nuclear weapons program.

With this validation, the NTRI formed an in-house commission dubbed the "Committee on Research in the Application of Nuclear Physics." After the humiliating defeat of the navy at the Battle of Midway in early June 1942, Admiral Isoroku Yamamoto seconded the motion and commanded the NTRI to construct new "epoch-making weapons" for the IJN. Ito drafted a proposal for this operation and submitted it to his superior officer at once. The new project, nicknamed the "B-Research Venture," was up and running by the end of the month, and it can be considered both a complementary venture to what would soon be known as the "Ni-Go Project," as well as a precursor to the upcoming F-Go Project. Once again, Nishina was selected to chair the NTRI nuclear physics committee, and a small starting sum of 2,000 yen (roughly $5,082 today) was allotted to them in funding.

The committee convened at least 10 times between July 1942 and March 1943, and Sagane, Kikuchi, Asada, and the 77-year-old Hantaro Nagaoka himself were among those regularly in attendance. During the second meeting, hosted a month after the inaugural conference, the attendees watched intently and scribbled away in their notebooks as Nishina drew a diagram of his take on a "heat engine" in real time. Plainly put, Nishina's apparatus was a kind of nuclear reactor designed to process a blend of enriched, highly concentrated Uranium-235 and heavy water. The committee members were conflicted. On the one hand, they applauded Nishina for the ingenuity of his design, which certainly seemed flawless on paper. On the other, they had no delusions about the abject difficulty of separating uranium isotopes and were intimidated by the mountainous pile of work that lay ahead of them. Asada, who prided himself on being a realist, reminded his peers to manage their expectations. American researchers, stated Asada, who were equipped with far more advanced hardware and technology, had only succeeded in splitting a piddling amount of Uranium-235 isotopes.

In the spring of 1941, upon perusing a year-old, battered copy of the *Nitrocellulose,* a German-language scientific journal, Lieutenant-Commander Tsutomu Murata from the Bureau of Ships (a department of the IJN) happened upon an astonishing headline: "America's Super-bomb." According to the fascinating article, American physicists were convinced that a single gram of Uranium-235 bombarded with slow neutrons was enough to trigger an earth-shattering blast. Captivated by these claims, Murata had the piece translated into Japanese and later circulated photocopies of the article to his colleagues at the Bureau and other naval divisions. Matao Mitsui and Megumu Iso, a pair of Bureau captains from the Artillery and Explosives department, shared Murata's enthusiasm. They, too, resolved to start their own separate project regarding the manufacturing of nuclear weapons. On June 14, 1941, Bunsaku Arakatsu, the Kyoto University physics professor previously based in Taiwan, was chosen to oversee the operation. Arakatsu's university team received 3,000 yen (approximately $143,000 today) in their first round of funding.

Arakatsu's team delivered the exhaustive report that Mitsui and Iso had ordered in September 1942. In brief, the researchers corroborated the article's claims and assured their superiors that nuclear chain reactions were certainly achievable with a proper facility and the right paraphernalia. On that note, Arakatsu admitted that the team, albeit nearly a year-and-a-half into the project, was still far away from accomplishing any of their goals. He urged the Bureau to take charge of or redirect the project to a more qualified party, as the venture was direly underfunded and the university laboratory lacked the personnel and elaborate tech required to achieve the objectives assigned to them in a timely manner. In a bid to keep Arakatsu on board, Bureau officials wired the university team an extra 5,000 yen, but this sum, while a nice gesture, was still a far cry from what they needed, and the project was therefore placed on the back burner for the time being.

In December 1942, the committee entrusted Kikuchi with the task of writing a letter to Ito, in which he delineated their plans to develop a pilot model of a "uranium nucleus fission energy utilization" machine, which they hoped would be operational by June 1945. The captain was taken aback by the unexpectedly lengthy estimated time of completion, and for an experimental apparatus, no less. He immediately ordered the committee, along with his own agents, to determine the statuses of the American and British nuclear weapons programs, particularly whether those nations were capable of creating an atomic bomb before the war's end, and whether Japan could beat them to the punch. Ito made his disappointment in the committee known, chiding the researchers for their lackadaisical attitudes and for intentionally being overly conservative with their calculations. The researchers took the flak, but at the end of the day, they knew their hands were tied.

In the report presented by the committee at their final meeting in March 1943, they reiterated that there was simply no way for Japan to construct a full-fledged atomic bomb in the foreseeable future, or in time to turn the tide of the war in their favor. With that said, their superiors could find comfort in the fact that all other global powers were lagging just as far, if not farther behind, and that "it [was] difficult even for the US to realize the application of atomic power during the war." As it turned out, that conjecture was woefully inaccurate.

Irked by the committee's intransigence and the mounting inconveniences of this intensely time-consuming project, Ito jettisoned the B-Research venture and disbanded the committee. The nuclear weapon programs of other nations were apparently still in their nascent stages anyway, Ito reasoned, so time was on their side. It made more sense for the NTRI to explore other possible innovations or more achievable options in the meantime. In the months that followed, NTRI researchers looked into proximity fuses, radar-based equipment, and the Tesla-inspired "Death Ray," an elephantine magnetron that would generate microwaves of several thousand kilowatts, which would then be concentrated through a reflecting mirror and trained on planes and other targets. Theoretically, humans directly exposed to these tissue-melting microwaves would be fried alive.

Following the committee's dissolution, Nishina returned to RIKEN full-time to resume work on the original project he had been assigned by Yasuda and Tojo. Japan was years, if not decades away from producing its first atomic bomb, but this was precisely why Nishina felt it imperative to expedite their investigations as much as possible, because, as he explained to his colleagues, it was their duty "to perform research to help Japan." Even if, in the worst case scenario, they failed to develop a nuclear-based explosive, the team could very well succeed in finding other non-military applications for nuclear power, which would still be beneficial to the empire in the long run.

Nishina's first order of business was to assign fixed roles to his subordinates so as to streamline their workflow. Takeuchi Masa was instructed to put his research on cosmic rays on hold and instead focus on assembling a Uranium-235 separator. Kunihiko Kigoshi was put in charge of the production of uranium-hexafluoride (a corrosive gaseous compound), which was then to be inserted into the separator and transformed into a gaseous state. Another physicist named Taketani Mitsuo, who was imprisoned for his Marxist publications and revolutionary activities, was also forced to contribute to their research on Uranium-235 separation while behind bars. The theoretical study of uranium nuclear chain reactions was delegated to Hidehiko Tamaki. As for Nishina, he picked up from where he left off and continued to work on the Calutron, which had been collecting dust in the corner of the lab, and set a tentative deadline of February 1944 for its completion.

Owing to their limited resources, the elementary state of their technology, and time restrictions, Nishina's team collectively concluded that the thermal diffusion technique – as opposed to gaseous diffusion, centrifugal separation, and electromagnetic separation methods – was their best bet. Their first major experiments with thermal diffusion and uranium-hexafluoride production called for the use of Clusius-Dickel column. This was a mechanism composed of two slender cylinders separated by a small gap and encased in a steel tower. Uranium-hexafluoride was to be heated inside these narrow cylinders, culminating in thermal convection; researchers could then collect the Uranium-235, a naturally occurring radioactive isotope deposited near the top of the tube. During this time, Tamaki calculated the critical mass for different quantities of condensed uranium moderated by water.

In the spring of 1943, Japanese officials worked themselves into a panic when they learned of the new speculations regarding the nuclear weapons development of enemy forces, which, contrary to the claims of local scientists, were supposedly progressing in leaps and bounds. Minister Tojo scheduled an emergency cabinet meeting, during which he made bitter remarks about the snail-like progress of Japan's atomic bomb research and commanded his subordinates to come up with ways to fast-track the empire's nuclear projects.

Many of the researchers resented Tojo for the undue pressure he imposed upon them, as well as being made to shoulder the blame for his inaction and lack of foresight, and quietly criticized the government's inability to provide them with the necessary capital and resources. In a 1995 interview with the *New York Times,* Suzuki, who had composed the 20-page report three years earlier, reflected on the team's low morale: "People like Mr. Tojo said we should hurry in our research. But he said that only after the war situation turned against Japan."

Furthermore, some junior researchers found their superiors rather difficult to work with and described some of their methods as tediously complex and unproductive, which, naturally, contributed to the inertia of their projects. Tamaki referred to this as "Tomonaga's Method of Boss Management" and explained, "Tomonaga advised me that even if [Nishina] suggested some outrageously time-consuming and difficult calculations, I should not say it was impossible on the spot...Once when they were in the library, they became so engrossed in discussion of a paper...that they forgot where they were and were shushed by the other researchers around them...The Boss's line of argument would often be, 'If this doesn't work, then, how about that?' As a result, outrageously complicated calculations sometimes came up in discussion...Tomonaga would never say 'no' to Nishina right away. He would just answer, 'I shall think about it.' Then he would work up an estimate and report to the Boss later that the calculation would require so many tens of thousands of pieces of calculation paper and take so many years. [Only then would] the Boss...be persuaded to drop the matter."

Nishina released a report of his newest findings in June 1943, in which he predicted that "a minimum amount of 10kg of 10% enriched uranium" would produce a massive shock of energy "equivalent to the energy released from an explosion of 18,000 tons of picric acid." Unbeknownst to the team, Nishina's calculations regarding the amount of explosive energy such a sample (in terms of critical mass) would generate were only partially accurate, because it is now known that uranium must be enriched to at least 90% to be classed as a weapons-grade substance. In addition, Nishina falsely believed that his "heat engine bomb" was capable of spawning this tremendous mass of energy. Neither Nishina nor his colleagues ever cottoned onto these pivotal errors, and they continued to maintain this fallacious train of thought throughout the development of their project.

On the morning of July 2, 1943, a pair of army officers – among them the team's chief liaison Major-General Nobuji – arrived at the RIKEN nuclear laboratory. Nishina disclosed his findings from the previous month and explained that the team required more rounds of funding so that they could complete the Calutron, among other tasks. The officers, vested with the authority to do so, pledged to provide the team with additional funds and resources. Nishina also rattled off a list of other requests. First, he suggested that the IJA and IJN to share their resources and create a cohesive plan for the advancement of the empire's atomic bomb project. His recommendation, unfortunately, was shot down on the spot, as these military branches were embroiled in a sticky rivalry and were therefore unwilling to cooperate with one another.

Nishina also asked the officers to send in an order to Berlin, by way of encrypted telegrams, for two tons of uranium ores. General Touransouke Kawashima transmitted the first telegram to the Japanese embassy in Berlin on July 7th. Berlin officials were understandably bewildered by the request, and replied a week later, inquired why Japan was so eager to acquire such a substantial amount of uranium.

Kawashima responded on August 24 that regardless of their alliance, he wanted to keep Germany in the dark about Japan's nuclear plans and claimed that the uranium was to be used in the production of synthetic aviation fuel for a non-existent underground project codenamed "Rogo Yaku." To Kawashima's chagrin, Berlin officials remained hesitant about sharing their limited uranium deposits, as they were producing uranium-based jet fuel themselves, and the Germans pressed the general for more details. Their aimless correspondence, which Allied cryptographers called "MAGIC decrypts," continued for several more months until November 18, when Kawashima, at long last, admitted the uranium was for Japan's atomic bomb ambitions. In the end, Berlin failed to deliver on this request until the final days of the war.

It was only in September 1943 that the IJA officially formalized Nishina's Uranium-235 thermal diffusion project and gave it a proper name: the "Ni-Go Project." What "Ni" stood for remains a subject of debate. Some believe the project was christened after the director of the enterprise, while others say it was derived from the venture's full name, *Nichi An* ("Sun Project")

The Ni-Go Project, as outlined by the *Atomic Heritage Foundation*, was centered on five "research themes," which were as follows: "atomic bomb theory, the separation of Uranium-235, the production of uranium-hexafluoride, the measurement of physical constraints, and the analysis of isotopes." The IJA injected a total of 700,000 yen (roughly $1.8 million today) into the project as funding and commissioned the construction of a new building at the RIKEN complex, which was simply referred to as "No. 49." Although the project was classified as a top-secret operation, Nishina's team was permitted to solicit advice from physicists across all local universities, who served as consultants on retainer.

The fresh facility and flashy new equipment notwithstanding, progress was met with stiff resistance. When the liaisons returned to RIKEN in February 1944, Nishina reported that both the Calutron and the Clusius column would be operational within a few days, but that they had hit a wall with the production of uranium-hexafluoride. They were running dangerously low on sugar – a highly sought-after, and therefore rare commodity during wartime – so much so that the researchers were forced to dip into their own paltry rations. Kigoshi, for one, shamefully revealed in a later interview that he had purloined his own mother's entire sugar supply.

The team's frustration intensified when the Calutron began to exhibit signs of wear and tear within months after its completion, and researchers were unable to obtain the "high-frequency-generating vacuum tubes" required for the machine to operate at full capacity. The Clusius column also started to malfunction two months later. Kigoshi was wrestling with issues of his own; his computations regarding the timing of nuclear chain reactions, for instance, was off by a factor of 10, a critical blunder that set them back by weeks.

By the time summer rolled around, the team had only managed to produce less than six ounces of uranium-hexafluoride, which was just enough to fuel a few rounds of experimentation. The liaisons, who swung by again on November 17, were greeted by more bad news. Due to the corrosion of the internal copper tubing, the Clusius column was bleeding uranium-hexafluoride gas at an alarming rate. Worse yet, the team was burning through cash at a breakneck pace. The team and its sponsors began to wonder if their mission, which was becoming increasingly costly by the minute, actually had any legs.

As one might expect, Nishina's patience was visibly wearing thin. It reached the point htat he began to disregard traditional etiquette and protocols. Japanese custom, for example, dictated that one must address their elders and superiors with the utmost deference at all times. When Major-General Nobuji innocently inquired why the researchers had not substituted the 10 kilograms of uranium needed for an atomic bomb with 10 kilograms of some other run-of-the-mill explosive, Nishina dismissed him with a brusque wave of his hand. "That's nonsense," he scoffed. Those who came to Nishina's defense insisted that he meant no disrespect, and that he had simply become accustomed to "the spirit of Copenhagen," or "a democratic style of research in which anyone could speak [their] mind."

In February 1945, Nishina and his colleagues rejoiced when they found that they had successfully generated another small batch of enriched uranium with the Clusius column – or so they thought. They chose to process the sample in the smaller cyclotron, bombarding it with neutrons in order to achieve nuclear fission, and their joy quickly proved to be a premature celebration. The test failed, and upon closer examination, it dawned on the researchers that the Clusius tube, in reality, had failed to separate almost any amount of Uranium-235 from the uranium-hexafluoride. Their worst fears, however, were yet to be realized.

In the early morning hours of March 10, 1945, a torrent of incendiary bombs unleashed by 330 American B-29 bombers rained down from the sky on Tokyo, laying waste to a quarter of the empire's capital and killing over 100,000 civilians. This attack, codenamed "Operation Meetinghouse," was among the deadliest air raids in World War II. The original laboratory, along with Building 49 at the RIKEN complex, were set alight by the roaring flames of the ensuing firestorm. Nishina's team stumbled out of their beds and raced to the scene, where they desperately attempted to extinguish the blaze with buckets of water, but all efforts were futile. By daybreak, both locations, as well as the Clusius column, had been completely incinerated. Luckily, the researchers managed to drag the two cyclotrons to safety in the nick of time, which, while slightly charred, were otherwise unscathed.

Over the next few days, the team sifted through the scorched leftovers of their work sites and tried to salvage whatever samples, testing materials, and equipment remained, but the future of the Ni-Go Project was looking increasingly bleak. The fire robbed them of their workstations, and they lost their entire stashes of uranium and heavy water.

In the wake of the deadly raid, the team brainstormed ways to keep the project afloat. Masa, the separator's engineer, produced a fresh set of calculations which suggested that light water was compatible with 5-10% enriched uranium, so the team elected to give this alternative a whirl.

As the RIKEN researchers conducted these light water trials, the IJA and IJN deployed an array of troops and volunteers to scour their colonies abroad for raw uranium. A crew was also sent to a local mine located in the small town of Ishikawite in the Fukushima prefecture, which housed the mainland's only notable collection of uranium deposits, but the reservoir was virtually depleted. The mining teams raked through uranium repositories in China and Mongolia, leaving no stone unturned, only to emerge more or less empty-handed.

Fortunately for the Japanese, the mining team in Burma (then Myanmar) fared better, given the abundance of alluvial Monazite sands along the Burmese rivers, which were replete with phosphorous, thorium, and uranium. The 250-mile tracks of the Siam-Burma Railway, which ran from the Thai district of Ban Pong to the Burmese town of Thanbyuzayat, were supposedly paved between 1940 and 1944 under Japanese command to facilitate the mining of uranium in these parts.

When all was said and done, the team at Burma only succeeded in harvesting at most a moderate amount of uranium due to the crew's disorganization and lack of mining expertise. According to a conflicting account, however, presented by the author of *Japan's Secret War* Robert K. Wilcox, the team transported at least 5,000 tons of uranium-oxide from Burma in 1943 alone. Readers must take Wilcox's work with a grain of salt, as the book is notorious among historians for its numerous unsubstantiated claims. The team stationed in Korea also managed to score a small pile of uranium, which provided researchers back home with only enough material for two or three small-scale experiments. At no point throughout the war did Japan hoard nearly enough uranium to manufacture an atomic bomb.

Then came a faint ray of hope, which went as quickly as it came. Berlin finally responded to the uranium order that Kawashima had placed back in the late spring of 1943. Instead of the two tons requested, however, German naval officers posted at the German-controlled Czech Republic loaded the *U-234* U-boat (a German type-XB submarine) with 1,235 pounds of unprocessed uranium-oxide. Lo and behold, the *U-234* did not set sail for Japan until a few days after Germany's declaration of surrender on May 7, and the submarine never reached its destination, as it was captured by American forces in the Atlantic a week later.

To evade capture, two Japanese lieutenant-commanders aboard the *U-234,* Hideo Tomonaga and Genzo Shoji, ingested poison tablets, and the officers' lifeless bodies were discovered on their bunk beds hours later. But the ship's entire cargo – which, aside from the 10 crates of uranium-oxide, consisted of lead, steel, mercury, brass, optical glass, diagrams of machinery, medical supplies, and an assortment of armaments – was promptly confiscated and catalogued by the American soldiers, and the uranium stockpile was transported to the diffusion plant in Oak Ridge. The Manhattan Project's researchers estimated that the uranium-oxide in the submarine would have generated roughly 7.7-lbs of Uranium-235, about 1/5 of the uranium required to produce a nuclear weapon.

The contention surrounding the nature and quality of the uranium seized on board, as well as Japan's intentions with the uranium in question, is worth noting. The radioactive crates allegedly bore the label "U-235," which some speculators claim is proof that the substances were to be converted into Uranium-235 and utilized in the production of an atomic bomb. Conversely, Japanese officials insisted that the tags were merely a mislabeling of the submarine's name, and that they had no plans of producing weapons-grade plutonium. Rather, the uranium-oxide was to be used in the manufacturing of synthetic methanol, a key ingredient in jet fuel. Moreover, it is now believed that the arrangement was purely a commercial transaction – there was no concrete evidence to suggest otherwise – and that Germany and Japan were in at no point collaborating with one another when it came to developing a nuclear weapon. Some have further speculated as to whether President Truman was aware of the uranium on the *U-234*, and if this information played a part in his decision to drop atomic bombs on Japan itself.

Either way, it wasn't the first time that Nishina's team was foiled by the US military. On June 24, 1944, a massive Japanese cargo submarine, the *I-52,* was torpedoed by American aircraft while en route to German-occupied Lorient, France. The attack sank the ship and killed all 99 crew members. The treasures aboard the *I-52,* which consisted of 120 tons of tin ingots, 146 gold bullions placed in metal cases (intended as payment for German optical technology), 60 tons of raw rubber, 11 tons of tungsten, 9.8 tons of molybdenum, 3.3 tons of quinine, three tons of opium, and 119 pounds of caffeine, sank with the submarine.

I-52 was originally scheduled to drop off the haul at Lorient and pick up 40 tons of cargo to be transported back to Japan, among which included a Jumo 213-A motor, multiple T-5 acoustic torpedoes, various chemicals, optical glass, steel, vacuum tubes, ball bearings, bomb-sights, radar equipment, a bale of confidential documents and diagrams, and finally, 1,760 pounds of uranium-oxide. Japanese researchers must have cringed at the thought of all the precious uranium that had slipped through their fingers.

The cards had been stacked against Nishina's team from the very beginning, and it would only be a matter of time before the entire house of cards came crashing down. On the afternoon of May 14, 1945, about an hour after news broke of *U-234*'s capture, Nishina called a meeting at one of the surviving buildings at RIKEN and somberly announced the end of the Ni-Go Project.

The operation was officially terminated by the IJA on June 28, and the team's research on nuclear weapons development was effectively discontinued.

Although the Ni-Go Project was finished, Nishina and his colleagues continued their experiments with uranium enrichment by way of thermal diffusion, albeit on a much smaller scale, and steered the bulk of their efforts towards exploring the non-military applications of nuclear power.

The F-Go Project

"I made efforts to swallow tears and to protect the species of the Japanese nation." – Emperor Hirohito

The end of Ni-Go did not spell the end of Japan's work on nuclear weapons, because the Japanese had not put all their eggs in one basket. In fact, nuclear research was also being carried out by Bunsaku Arakatsu and the Bureau of Ships.

There are several reasons why Arakatsu is regarded as one of the most influential nuclear physicists to emerge from Japan during the era, perhaps second only to Nishina. By all accounts, Arakatsu was the perfect candidate for the job. For starters, like Nishina, Professor Arakatsu pursued a higher education in Europe in the 1920s, first studying at Berlin University as a pupil and later friend of Albert Einstein, then the Technische Hochschule in Zurich, and finally, the Cavendish Laboratory at Cambridge. His work with the disintegration of light nuclei aside, Arakatsu, once again like Nishina, went on to build his own working cyclotron in 1941.

The IJN initially delved into nuclear power – then a fledgling, esoteric science – to discern if it was a viable energy source for warships and other naval vessels, as the navy was in urgent need of a petroleum substitute after the oil embargo was foisted upon Japan. It was that fateful article that Lieutenant-Commander Murata happened upon in the *Nitrocellulose* that sparked the navy's interest in the development of nuclear weapons, which segued into the Bureau of Ship's atomic energy project. This is not to be confused with the short-lived committee commissioned by the NTRI, which was a separate naval operation. As a matter of fact, the committee, including Nishina himself, was deliberately kept out of the loop, and thus it remained unaware of Arakatsu's project for two years.

The Bureau's project was formally resuscitated in May 1943, not long after the department's foreign intelligence agents dug up credible intel concerning the rapid progression of the United States' nuclear weapons program. Once everything was settled on, Arakatsu and his team at Kyoto University were presented with 350,000 yen (equivalent to $810,000 today) up front. In other accounts, the team was granted as much as 600,000 yen ($1.39 million), which was appreciably more than the pitiful 8,000 yen the team had no choice but to make do with two years earlier.

The operation was officially titled the "F-Go Project." Similar to the moniker attached to Nishina's project, what the "F" in "F-Go" stood for remains open to question. Some say the "F" represented "fluoride," as in "uranium-hexafluoride"; others say the "F" was short for "fission." In contrast to the thermal diffusion method of the Ni-Go Project, the F-Go operation banked on gaseous uranium centrifuges, which Arakatsu's team believed were superior vehicles for Uranium-235 isotope separation.

Arakatsu was to report directly to Rear Admiral Nitta Shigeru and Lieutenant-Commander Kitagawa Tetsuzo; the extent of Murata's involvement following the revival of the project is unclear. At the university lab, Arakatsu's number two was a young, bright-eyed master's student by the name of Sakae Shimuzu, who was 25 years his junior. Other noteworthy members of Arakatsu's team included future Nobel Laureate and Nishina's former mentee Dr. Yukawa; RIKEN researcher Dr. Asao Sugimoto; particle and theoretical physics expert from Osaka University Dr. Minoru Kobayashi; and Dr. Shoichi Sakata, the man behind the aptly named "Sakata model," the PMNS matrix, the two-meson theory, and the much-touted *Theoretical Physics and Dialetics of Nature* (1947).

Strangely enough, while Arakatsu and Nishina shared mutual goals, their physical interactions numbered no more than a handful of times. One of these rare face-to-face meetings transpired in late 1943, when Arakatsu and other eminent names in the field dropped in at RIKEN to marvel at the pristine new equipment within the recently erected Building 49. Shortly after the tour, Arakatsu and Nishina retired to a corner and briefly compared notes on the isotopic separation of uranium.

The internal strife within the military branches, in particular the deep-rooted tensions between the IJA and the IJN, undoubtedly impeded the progress of Japan's atomic bomb project. It wasn't until the autumn of 1944 that the branches finally cast aside their differences and joined forces in the name of advancing the empire's nuclear knowledge. To inaugurate the long-awaited alliance between these branches, the Army-Navy Technology Enforcement Committee was established. Bureau Captain Mitsui, who had co-founded the first version of the F-Go Project, was tasked with overseeing the general planning of this collaboration.

Much to the dismay of all researchers involved, it was anything but smooth sailing from there on out. The IJA and the IJN failed to see eye to eye on budget issues, investigative techniques, and research priorities, among other matters. But at last, after more than a year of aimless negotiations, the bickering branches arrived at a compromise. In the spring of 1945, IJN officials conceded that the research conducted at RIKEN was more extensive, and the knowledge and technical skills of its personnel of a higher caliber, when compared to those at Kyoto University. The Navy, and to that effect, Arakatsu's team, agreed to play second fiddle to Nishina's crew. As such, while Arakatsu's team would continue with their own studies on centrifuges, they were to give precedence to providing support to the RIKEN researchers whenever necessary.

Distracted by the side projects constantly assigned to them by RIKEN scientists, Arakatsu's team found it woefully difficult to even lay the groundwork for their research on centrifugal separation, a process otherwise known as "ultracentrifugation."

The work was painfully slow, but Arakatsu eventually finished the first draft of his blueprints for an ultra-centrifuge, which was designed to spin at 60,000-rpm. The *Radioactivity* website, supported by the French Institute of Nuclear Physics and Particle Physics and EDP-Sciences, explains the mechanics of ultracentrifugation in the following passage: "Basically, centrifuges can be used to enrich uranium for reactors...or to fabricate weapons-grade uranium...The process involves feeding (gaseous) uranium-hexafluoride in an ultra-centrifuge spinning at high speed. The heavier uranium atoms (U-238) migrate to the periphery of the machine while the lightest (U-235) migrate preferentially towards its axis. Uranium atoms near and not near the axis are pumped separately and sent to another centrifuge...To achieve a significant enrichment, gas must pass through thousands of centrifuges arranged in cascades...[Today,] production units can be quite small and energy needs are reasonable, 50 times lower than gaseous diffusion...For uranium enriched to 90% that goes into the making of [nuclear] bombs, one just needs to continue the enrichment well beyond the 4% requested for reactor fuels."

Arakatsu and his accelerator

A treatise titled "Ultracentrifugal Separation," authored by Shimuzu and published in November 1944, expanded on the team's arguments for this method, and documented the team's experiments with Uranium-235 enrichment and isotopic separation.

As reported by the Manhattan Project Intelligence Committee in later years, F-Go researchers allegedly secured an average of 20 grams of heavy water every month from the multifaceted Korean Hydro-Electric Company in Hungnam (formerly Konan). Founded by Jun Noguchi in 1926, the plant started out as a manufacturer for electrolytic ammonia used in fertilizer before installing a heavy water SKU (a byproduct of ammonia) sometime in the following decade.

In the mid-1940s, the Japanese Navy also organized a series of independent missions to China for the purpose of expanding, or at the very least replenishing Arakatsu's, as well as the IJN's personal supplies of uranium ore. When their mining efforts fell flat, Japanese officers resorted to swiping uranium-oxide from the caches of the Chinese Navy in Shanghai, and from the stores of Chinese ceramics factories. Reports show that Lieutenant-Commander Miroshi Ishiwatari was selected to lead the search on uranium-oxide specifically for the F-Go Project between March and May 1944. The uranium ores amassed on this quest were then delivered to the Kyoto University lab to be assayed by Dr. Kumura Kiichi of the F-Go team.

By the fall of 1944, the Japanese military's confidence in the atomic bomb project was fast waning. As the Ni-Go & F-Go teams plodded on with their research, senior officials started to experiment with other forms of unorthodox weapons. In one of their more peculiar operations, Japanese technicians attached explosive devices to paraffin balloons, which were then loaded onto military planes and released over American and Canadian terrain. It should come as no surprise that most of the 9,000 balloon bombs launched proved to be duds, as they either crashed into sea and unpopulated areas or failed to detonate altogether. Even more bizarre was a suicide bombing scheme involving a submarine and a light aircraft, which were to be packed with plague-riddled fleas, destined for San Diego. Mercifully, the end of the war prevented this plot from ever being executed. These unusual and impractical side quests – considering the time, energy, and resources squandered on these fruitless operations – did nothing to help the stagnancy of Japan's atomic bomb research.

Sometime between the winter of 1944 and early 1945, the Bureau wired the F-Go team an extra 300,000 yen in funding. To the Bureau's exasperation, the handsome sum did little to enhance the productivity of Arakatsu and his colleagues. With the war drawing to a close and the Axis hanging by a fine thread, motivation levels were tailing off with each passing day. Like the Ni-Go crew, the F-Go team had accepted the fact that they were, at best, a decade away from mastering the atomic bomb, and they were now merely going through the motions to keep their superiors satisfied. By then, Arakatsu, who had only finished ironing out the kinks of his design and had not yet even begun to develop a prototype for his ultra-centrifuge, was running seriously behind schedule. Even if he had started construction for the first model on time, it would not have been completed until August at the earliest.

Wilcox, however, begged to differ. According to Wilcox, not only did Arakatsu actually complete his prototype, the F-Go team had struck a deal with the Hokushine Electric Company, the Tokyo Keiki Electric Company, and the Sumitomo engineering firm for the construction of an even larger ultra-centrifuge. This prodigious piece of machinery was to be fitted with delicate carbon fiber brushes and powerful rotor drums fashioned from "rare earth metal alloys," and it would be calibrated to spin at the dizzying speed of 100,000 to 150,000-RPM. If such an order was placed, this overambitious design would have been unattainable even by today's standards, as the most sophisticated centrifuges in this day and age can only spin at a speed of approximately 50,000-RPM.

The F-Go researchers and their sponsors convened for the last time on July 21, 1945. During the session, Arakatsu's team relayed to their superiors what they (and Nishina's crew) had known from the very beginning: the production of an atomic bomb before the war's end was simply not possible. Although Arakatsu's team would also continue to contribute to the general research of nuclear power in their own capacity without the financial support of the IJN, this admission by the F-Go team, followed by the official announcement of the project's disbandment a week later, marked the end of the empire's nuclear weapons program during the war.

The Work after the War

"We learn little from victory, much from defeat." – ancient Japanese proverb

As the saying goes, hindsight is 20/20, and historians still debate whether Japan truly set out to build and actually deploy an atomic bomb. For their part, the Americans certainly seemed to think the Japanese were attempting to build one, and as late as February 1945, the Office of Strategic Services sounded alarms when officials distributed a report regarding their concerns about an impending "atomic discharge to be used against Allied aircraft." This sentiment is also echoed by most experts today.

Most of those directly involved in the Ni-Go and F-Go projects, on the other hand, took great exception to these claims. Nishina, for one, contended that he personally never intended to construct a nuclear weapon. He claimed that he had agreed to spearhead the project under false pretenses – namely, that he accepted the position to obtain the funds and resources required to complete his unfinished Calutron, and to quench his own curiosity around nuclear power. The only reason he chose to maintain the facade, said Nishina, was to keep up appearances both at home and with his foreign contemporaries. Japanese scientists who survived the war, he explained, would have "lost face" if their "research [during the war] appeared too meager." Some theorized that Nishina may have also done so to bail out his young peers, who would have been forced to enlist had they not been involved in nuclear research.

When asked to defend their actions, NTRI Captain Ito and Lieutenant-Colonel Suzuki responded in similar fashion. Ito claimed that the Committee's research revolved solely around investigating the feasibility of uranium-based weapons, so that the empire could bolster their defenses and employ the necessary precautions, should they become the target of a nuclear attack. Suzuki took a different approach for his defense; he insisted that even if Japan had succeeded in squirreling away the uranium-oxide needed for an atomic bomb, the enrichment and separation capabilities of their primitive and defective tech were severely limited. Despite what official reports and hearsay suggested, Suzuki claimed that WWII-era Japanese scientists were only able to produce one piddling milligram of "usable uranium" every year. Suzuki concluded, "At this rate, it would [have taken] 10,000 years to produce a bomb."

As it turned out, the US military's thoughts on the motivations behind Japan's atomic bomb project proved to be irrelevant, and just weeks after the termination of Japan's nuclear weapons program, the residents of Hiroshima and Nagasaki became the victims of the only nuclear attacks to date. The first atomic bomb, nicknamed "Little Boy," was discharged over Hiroshima by the B-29 bomber *Enola Gay*, and the 13-kiloton blast obliterated five square miles of the city in one fell swoop. An estimated 60,000 to 80,000 civilians were killed immediately, and tens of thousands more later perished from radiation exposure. "Fat Man" was unleashed on Nagasaki three days later, claiming the lives of another 40,000 civilians. All in all, as many as 226,000 lost their lives.

At first, the shell-shocked Japanese, once again ignoring the conclusions of the Ni-Go and F-Go teams, called for the resurrection of these projects and ordered the researchers to manufacture a nuclear bomb packed with a blast of equal proportions within six months. When Japan finally resigned itself to the dark reality of defeat, Emperor Hirohito swallowed his pride and raised the white flag. The day of Japan's surrender, August 15, has since been commemorated as "Victory over Japan Day," or "V-J Day" for short.

From that point forward, Japanese scientists directed their research towards the impact and damage inflicted by atomic bombs, as well as the immediate and long-term effects of radiation exposure. Nishina was among the first to be summoned to examine the bomb site at Hiroshima. He was reportedly so overwhelmed with remorse about his misjudgment of America's nuclear weapons research that he had to be talked out of committing suicide.

Meanwhile, the Americans dispatched an intelligence team to Japan on the day of their surrender, partly to help clean up the wreckage and partly to analyze the state of Japan's nuclear weapons program. Chief of Foreign Intelligence for the Manhattan Engineer District Robert Furman appeared to have been somewhat unimpressed by Japan's progress, as evidenced by a 2008 interview: "Don't forget, if they had a project, we knew it would have to be a tremendous project like Oak Ridge. If somebody showed us a 40,000-ft warehouse and said that was their project, why, we felt pretty safe because Oak Ridge was a million feet...half the size of the state of Rhode Island. As far as we knew, nobody could do it any quicker or any faster...From this, we could make our report back that there was no serious project. I think that report has stood up under questioning over the years. Every once in a while, someone wants to write an article saying a secret plant was producing atomic bombs. This we could easily check out and force them to remove the report."

The Manhattan Project Intelligence Committee came to a similar conclusion: "The same lack of sufficient high-quality uranium that had impeded the German atomic bomb project had also, as it turned out, obstructed Japanese attempts to make a bomb."

In October 1945, Nishina appealed to the American forces still stationed in Japan for permission to fire up his cyclotrons at RIKEN so that he could conduct experiments for "biological and medical research." American officials initially gave Nishina the approval to proceed with his nuclear studies, but by November 10, they had changed their tune. Acting on the direct orders of Secretary of War Robert P. Patterson, American soldiers commandeered the five cyclotrons from the laboratories at RIKEN, Osaka University, and Kyoto University. On November 24, American troops theatrically disassembled the cyclotrons before a great audience and then chucked the bits and pieces into the Gulf of Tokyo.

Needless to say, the former members of the Ni-Go and F-Go teams took great offense to the seizure of their equipment, especially considering the comments made by General Leslie Groves, who referred to Nishina's Calutron as a useless "white elephant" in terms of atomic bomb production. They were also dismayed by the government's choice to making a spectacle of the situation for the sake of optics. Equipment, notebooks, confidential reports, and other key documents pertaining to the Ni-Go and F-Go projects were also seized, which were then either destroyed or stowed away in American archives.

A picture of Arakatsu's equipment being disassembled

On October 2, 1946, an article published in the *Atlanta Constitution*, titled "Actual Test Was Success," caused a ripple of panic across the United States. Its author, David Snell, reported that contrary to popular belief, Japan had built an atomic bomb called the "*genzai bakuden*," and had successfully tested the nuclear explosive on an island 20 miles off the Korean coast on August 10, less than 24 hours after the bombing of Nagasaki. This intel, Snell claimed, came from a Japanese officer, only identified by his alias, "Captain Wakabayashi," who had allegedly witnessed the blast firsthand. The Japanese staunchly denied these allegations, and experts did not find these claims credible.

In the years immediately following the devastating nuclear attacks, Japan openly swore off all forms of nuclear weapons and vowed never to produce or purchase such explosives. Lawmakers passed the Basic Atomic Energy Law in 1956, a binding policy that restricted the research, development, and utilization of nuclear energy on Japanese grounds to civilian purposes. On February 5, 1968, Prime Minister Eisaku Sato publicly pledged, on behalf of Japan, to uphold the Three Non-Nuclear Principles: "non-possession, non-production, [and] non-introduction of nuclear weapons on its territory." Japanese representatives signed the Nuclear Non-Proliferation Treaty eight years later.

In the decades since the war, Japan's nuclear infrastructure has improved dramatically, so much so that experts believe it now possesses the ability to produce atomic bombs and other nuclear armaments with ease should they choose to do so. For the most part, the current government has repeatedly reassured the public that they have no plans of reversing its stringent demilitarization and nuclear non-weaponization policies, and Japan seems content with remaining under the so-called nuclear umbrella of the United States. That said, in light of the recurring nuclear threats posed by rogue states such as North Korea, a few politicians and military officials, including Defense Minister Shigeru Ishiban, are strongly urging the government to reconsider.

In January 2021, Japan made headlines again when its leaders revealed their reluctance to sign off on the UN's Treaty on the Prohibition of Nuclear Weapons. Prime Minister Yoshihide Suga explained the stance: "The Treaty...does not have the support of nuclear weapons states, nor many non-nuclear weapons states. In line with our position that it is necessary to pursue a steady and realistic path towards nuclear disarmament, Japan has no intention of signing the treaty." Akiyama Nobumasa, a nuclear security policy professor at Hitotsubashi University, added, "Joining the ban treaty is like trying to achieve perfection. But by signing this treaty, how are we going to achieve the goal of pressuring nuclear states to give up nuclear weapons? The humanitarian element is only part of it. The national security context for every country is different, and the TPNW approach to banning weapons altogether is a catch-all discourse."

Online Resources

Other World War II titles by Charles River Editors

Further Reading

Adelstein, J., & Yamamoto, M. (2019, August 6). What If, in World War II, Japan Got the Atomic Bomb First? Retrieved February 28, 2021, from https://www.thedailybeast.com/in-world-war-ii-what-if-japan-got-the-atomic-bomb-first

Aftergood, S., & Garbose, J. (2012, June 1). Nuclear Weapons Program. Retrieved February 28, 2021, from https://fas.org/nuke/guide/japan/nuke/

Atsushi, K. (2019, July 10). Japan's Industrial Revolution. Retrieved February 28, 2021, from https://www.nippon.com/en/japan-topics/b06904/japan%E2%80%99s-industrial-revolution.html

Ballaban, M. (2015, August 5). New Documents Found Pointing To Japan's WWII Atomic Bomb Program. Retrieved February 28, 2021, from https://foxtrotalpha.jalopnik.com/new-documents-found-pointing-to-japanese-atomic-bomb-pr-1722338915

Barnhart, M. A. (1988). *Japan Prepares for Total War: The Search for Economic Security, 1919–1941 (Cornell Studies in Security Affairs)*. Cornell University Press.

Boyd, E. (2020, August 4). WHAT EVER BECAME OF THE I-52? (AND ITS TWO TONS OF GOLD?). Retrieved February 28, 2021, from https://numa.net/2020/08/what-ever-became-of-the-i-52-and-its-two-tons-of-gold/

Broad, W. J. (1995, December 31). Captured Cargo, Captivating Mystery. Retrieved February 28, 2021, from https://www.nytimes.com/1995/12/31/us/captured-cargo-captivating-mystery.html

Broad, W. J. (1995, July 18). Lost Japanese Sub With 2 Tons of Axis Gold Found on Floor of Atlantic. Retrieved February 28, 2021, from https://www.nytimes.com/1995/07/18/science/lost-japanese-sub-with-2-tons-of-axis-gold-found-on-floor-of-atlantic.html

Brown, L. M., & Nambu, Y. (2008, October 7). A History of Nobel Physicists from Wartime Japan. Retrieved February 28, 2021, from https://www.scientificamerican.com/article/physicists-in-wartime-japan/

Burton, K. D. (2020, July 16). "Destroyer of Worlds": The Making of an Atomic Bomb. Retrieved February 28, 2021, from https://www.nationalww2museum.org/war/articles/making-the-atomic-bomb-trinity-test

Chen, C. P. (2010, October). Yoshio Nishina. Retrieved February 28, 2021, from https://ww2db.com/person_bio.php?person_id=605

Editors, A. H. (2016, May 25). Japanese Atomic Bomb Project. Retrieved February 28, 2021, from https://www.atomicheritage.org/history/japanese-atomic-bomb-project

Editors, B. B. (2018, August 28). WW2 prisoners died building a railway for the Japanese. Retrieved February 28, 2021, from https://www.bbc.com/news/av/stories-45334160

Editors, C. U. (2020). Japan's Foreign Relations and Role in the Late 20th Century. Retrieved February 28, 2021, from http://afe.easia.columbia.edu/special/japan_1950_foreign_relations.htm

Editors, D. W. (2018). Japan and the industrial boom of 1917. Retrieved February 28, 2021, from https://www.dw.com/en/japan-and-the-industrial-boom-of-1917/a-39936520

Editors, E. N. (2017). 3. Japan's nuclear projects. Retrieved February 28, 201, from https://erenow.net/ww/hiroshima-the-worlds-bomb/14.php

Editors, F. D. (2012, November). JAPAN IN THE EARLY 20TH CENTURY. Retrieved February 28, 2021, from http://factsanddetails.com/japan/cat16/sub108/item510.html

Editors, G. K. (2013). Great Kanto Earthquake of 1923. Retrieved February 28, 2021, from http://www.greatkantoearthquake.com/aftermath.html

Editors, G. S. (2011). Japan - 1912-1952 - Early 20th Century. Retrieved February 28, 2021, from https://www.globalsecurity.org/military/world/japan/history-20c.htm

Editors, H. C. (2019, December 2). Arms Race. Retrieved February 28, 2021, from https://www.history.com/topics/cold-war/arms-race

Editors, H. C. (2020, February 21). Atomic Bomb History. Retrieved February 28, 2021, from https://www.history.com/topics/world-war-ii/atomic-bomb-history

Editors, H. C. (2020, July 24). United States freezes Japanese assets. Retrieved February 28, 2021, from https://www.history.com/this-day-in-history/united-states-freezes-japanese-assets

Editors, H. J. (2020, January 28). A Brief History of Japan from the Late 19th Century to the Early 20th Century. Retrieved February 28, 2021, from https://heartlandjapan.com/a-brief-history-of-japan-from-the-late-19th-century-to-the-early-20th-century/

Editors, H. S. (2017). Japan, China, the United States and the Road to Pearl Harbor, 1937–41. Retrieved February 28, 2021, from https://history.state.gov/milestones/1937-1945/pearl-harbor

Editors, N. B. (2021). Factsheet: Japan and Nuclear Weapons – A complicated timeline. Retrieved February 28, 2021, from https://www.icanw.org/factsheet_japan_and_nuclear_weapons_a_complicated_timeline

Editors, N. M. (2020). Cockcroft-Walton generator. Retrieved February 21, 2021, from https://www.nms.ac.uk/explore-our-collections/stories/science-and-technology/cockcroft-walton-generator/

Editors, O. U. (2019). The Story of the Atomic Bomb. Retrieved February 28, 2021, from https://ehistory.osu.edu/articles/story-atomic-bomb

Editors, P. C. (2015). Survey activities by the War Department Hiroshima Damage Survey Team. Retrieved February 28, 2021, from http://www.pcf.city.hiroshima.jp/virtual/VirtualMuseum_e/exhibit_e/exh0307_e/exh03075_e.html

Editors, R. (2020). RIKEN - Historical Figures. Retrieved February 28, 2021, from https://www.riken.jp/en/about/history/figures/

Editors, R. (2020). Ultracentrifugation. Retrieved February 28, 2021, from https://www.radioactivity.eu.com/site/pages/Ultracentrifugation.htm

Editors, S. S. (2020). Cockcroft and Walton accelerator. Retrieved February 28, 2021, from https://scientificsentence.net/Equations/Nuclear_Physics/index.php?key=yes&Integer=cockcroft _walton_accelerator

Editors, W. (2020, December 17). Bunsaku Arakatsu. Retrieved February 28, 2021, from https://en.wikipedia.org/wiki/Bunsaku_Arakatsu

Editors, W. (2021, February 8). Japanese nuclear weapon program. Retrieved February 28, 2021, from https://en.wikipedia.org/wiki/Japanese_nuclear_weapon_program

Edwards, G. (2014, June 2). How the Dreadnought sparked the 20th Century's first arms race. Retrieved February 28, 2021, from https://www.bbc.com/news/magazine-27641717

Edwards, G., PhD. (2007, June). Speaker's Notes for the Nunavut Planning Commission Gordon Edwards Ph.D. Retrieved February 28, 2021, from http://www.ccnr.org/Baker_Lake_summary.pdf

Frame, P. W. (2018). —Tales from the Atomic Age—. Retrieved February 28, 2021, from https://www.orau.org/ptp/articlesstories/u234.htm

Fukuki, S. (1991). Shell-Like Structure of Nuclei Introduced by Tadayoshi Hikosaka in 1934. Retrieved February 28, 2021, from https://watanaby.files.wordpress.com/2013/03/fukui-2.pdf

Grunden, W., Walker, M., & Yamnazaki, M. (2005). Wartime Nuclear Weapons Research in Germany and Japan. Retrieved February 28, 2021, from https://www.researchgate.net/publication/44631522_Wartime_Nuclear_Weapons_Research_in_ Germany_and_Japan

Gunson, S. (2009). Japan's A-Bomb project. Retrieved February 28, 2021, from https://sites.google.com/site/naziabomb/home/japan-s-a-bomb-project

Hall, I. (2016, July 13). U-234, Hitler's Last U-Boat... The Hail-Mary Pass to Japan. Retrieved February 28, 2021, from http://ianhallauthor.blogspot.com/2016/07/u-234-hitlers-last-u-boat-hail-mary.html

Hayashi, Y. (2019). Japanese Militarism. Retrieved February 28, 2021, from https://graphics.wsj.com/100-legacies-from-world-war-1/japanese-militarism

Higgs, R. (2006, May 1). How U.S. Economic Warfare Provoked Japan's Attack on Pearl Harbor. Retrieved February 28, 2021, from https://www.independent.org/news/article.asp?id=1930

Huffman, J. (2021). The Meiji Restoration Era, 1868-1889. Retrieved February 28, 2021, from https://aboutjapan.japansociety.org/the_meiji_restoration_era_1868-1889

Hulme, K. (2017, December 20). The Horrific Story of Thailand's Death Railway. Retrieved February 28, 2021, from https://theculturetrip.com/asia/thailand/articles/the-story-behind-the-death-railyways-horrendous-past-in-thailand/

Hutchinson, S. (2015, June 30). THE JAPANESE ALMOST BUILT ATOMIC BOMBS DURING WORLD WAR II. Retrieved February 28, 2021, from https://www.inverse.com/article/4170-the-japanese-almost-built-atomic-bombs-during-world-war-ii

Hyodo, N. (1996, October). A Plan To Deploy Nuclear Warheads in Japan. Retrieved February 28, 2021, from https://fas.org/nuke/guide/japan/missile/FBIS-EAS-96-227.htm

Inamura, T. T. (2016, April 11). Nagaoka's atomic model and hyperfine interactions. Retrieved February 28, 2021, from https://www.ncbi.nlm.nih.gov/pmc/articles/PMC4989051/

Kenny, J. (2017, November 2). Rutherford's Legacy – the birth of nuclear physics in Manchester. Retrieved February 28, 2021, from https://www.manchester.ac.uk/discover/news/rutherfords-legacy--the-birth-of-nuclear-physics-in-manchester/#:~:text=Manchester%20is%20the%20birthplace%20of,in%20laboratories%20at%20the%20University.

Khaliq, R. U. (2021, January 22). Japan doubtful about nuclear ban treaty. Retrieved February 28, 2021, from https://www.aa.com.tr/en/asia-pacific/japan-doubtful-about-nuclear-ban-treaty/2119109#:~:text=Tokyo%20questions%20effectiveness%20of%20UN's,participation%20by%20nuclear%2Darmed%20countries&text=Raising%20questions%20about%20its%20effectiveness,with%2050%20members%20ratifying%20it.

Kim, D. W. (2007). *Yoshio Nishina: Father of Modern Physics in Japan*. CRC Press.

Kristof, N. D. (1995, August 8). Japan's A-Bomb Project: One of War's 'What Ifs'. Retrieved February 28, 2021, from https://www.nytimes.com/1995/08/08/world/japan-s-a-bomb-project-one-of-war-s-what-ifs.html

Kulacki, G. (2020, May 1). Does Japan Have Nuclear Weapons? Retrieved February 28, 2021, from https://allthingsnuclear.org/gkulacki/does-japan-have-nuclear-weapons

Little, B. (2018, August 31). "Father of the Atomic Bomb" Was Blacklisted for Opposing H-Bomb. Retrieved February 28, 2021, from https://www.history.com/news/father-of-the-atomic-bomb-was-blacklisted-for-opposing-h-bomb

Long, T. (2011, March 9). March 9, 1945: Burning the Heart Out of the Enemy. Retrieved February 28, 2021, from https://www.wired.com/2011/03/0309incendiary-bombs-kill-100000-tokyo/

Low, M. (2005). *Science and the Building of a New Japan*. Springer.

Mahaffey, J. (2017). *Atomic Adventures*. Simon and Schuster.

Melzer, J. (2017, October 19). Warfare 1914-1918 (JAPAN). Retrieved February 28, 2021, from https://encyclopedia.1914-1918-online.net/article/warfare_1914-1918_japan

Nagase-Reimer, K., Grunden, W., & Yamazaki, M. (2005, January). Nuclear Weapons Research in Japan During the Second World War. Retrieved February 28, 2021, from https://www.researchgate.net/publication/327076517_Nuclear_Weapons_Research_in_Japan_During_the_Second_World_War

Ofek, R. (2018, March 18). Is Japan Considering Joining the Nuclear Arms Race? Retrieved February 28, 2021, from https://besacenter.org/perspectives-papers/is-japan-considering-joining-the-nuclear-arms-race/

Paschoa, A. S. (1997, January 15). RADIOACTIVITY IN THE TWENTIETH CENTURY AND SOME OF ITS IMPLICATIONS FOR THE THIRD MILLENIUM. Retrieved February 28, 2021, from https://www.ipen.br/biblioteca/cd/sgna/1997/ANS.HTM

Pike, S. (2019, March 27). What is the difference between pure and enriched uranium? Retrieved February 28, 2021, from https://www.argonelectronics.com/blog/what-is-the-difference-between-pure-and-enriched-uranium

Ragbeb, M. (2020, December 23). Japanese Nuclear Weapons Program. Retrieved February 28, 2021, from https://mragheb.com/NPRE%20402%20ME%20405%20Nuclear%20Power%20Engineering/Japanese%20Nuclear%20Weapons%20Program.pdf

Ray, M. (2021, February 1). Russo-Japanese War. Retrieved from https://www.britannica.com/event/Russo-Japanese-War

Ryall, J. (2015, July 1). Was Japan building a nuclear bomb? Notebooks uncovered in Kyoto show how far wartime scientists had got. Retrieved February 28, 2021, from https://www.scmp.com/news/asia/article/1830460/discovered-notebooks-show-how-close-japan-got-acquiring-nuclear-bomb

Samuel, W. W. (2004). *American Raiders: The Race to Capture the Luftwaffe's Secrets*. University Press of Mississippi.

Schwarzer, R. (2020, December 1). An introduction to EBSD Backscatter Kikuchi Diffraction in the Scanning Electron Microscope. Retrieved February 28, 2021, from http://www.ebsd.info/

Sirpala, T. (2021, February 10). Japan's Dilemma Over Nuclear Disarmament. Retrieved February 28, 2021, from https://thediplomat.com/2021/02/japans-dilemma-over-nuclear-disarmament/

Snell, D. (1946). Japan Developed Atom Bomb; Russia Grabbed Scientists. Retrieved February 28, 2021, from http://www.reformation.org/atlanta-constitution.html

Sovacool, B. K., & Valentine, S. V. (2012). *The National Politics of Nuclear Power: Economics, Security, and Governance*. Routledge.

Wellerstein, A. (2020, August 4). Did the U.S. plan to drop more than two atomic bombs on Japan? Retrieved February 28, 2021, from https://www.nationalgeographic.com/history/world-history-magazine/article/did-united-states-plan-drop-more-than-two-atomic-bombs-japan

Windrem, R. (2014, March 11). Japan Has Nuclear 'Bomb in the Basement,' and China Isn't Happy. Retrieved February 28, 2021, from https://www.nbcnews.com/storyline/fukushima-anniversary/japan-has-nuclear-bomb-basement-china-isn-t-happy-n48976

Winn, P. (2019, March 14). Japan has plutonium, rockets and rivals. Will it ever build a nuke? Retrieved February 28, 2021, from https://interactive.pri.org/2019/03/japan-nuclear/index.html

Woolbright, S., Schumacher, J., & Michonova, E. (2014, January). From the Dawn of Nuclear Physics to the First Atomic Bombs. Retrieved February 28, 2021, from https://www.researchgate.net/publication/260249828_From_the_Dawn_of_Nuclear_Physics_to_the_First_Atomic_Bombs#pf9

Yanes, J. (2017, February 17). Oppenheimer, from the Atomic Bomb to Pacifism. Retrieved February 28, 2021, from https://www.bbvaopenmind.com/en/science/physics/oppenheimer-from-the-atomic-bomb-to-pacifism/

Free Books by Charles River Editors

We have brand new titles available for free most days of the week. To see which of our titles are currently free, click on this link.

Discounted Books by Charles River Editors

We have titles at a discount price of just 99 cents everyday. To see which of our titles are currently 99 cents, click on this link.

Made in the USA
Monee, IL
14 August 2023

41035680R00026